BEN & MARK

Boys of the High Country

THIS BOOK BELONGS TO

_____

_____

BEN & MARK
Boys of the High Country

Christine Fernyhough & John Bougen

RANDOM HOUSE
NEW ZEALAND

A RANDOM HOUSE BOOK published by Random House New Zealand
18 Poland Road, Glenfield, Auckland, New Zealand

For more information about our titles go to www.randomhouse.co.nz

A catalogue record for this book is available from the National
Library of New Zealand

Random House New Zealand is part of the Random House Group
New York   London   Sydney   Auckland   Delhi   Johannesburg

First published 2009. Reprinted 2009 (three times)

© 2009 text Christine Fernyhough; photographs John Bougen

The moral rights of the authors have been asserted

ISBN 978 1 86979 068 4

Design: Anna Seabrook
Maps: Imogen Tunnicliffe
Printed in China by Everbest Printing Co Ltd

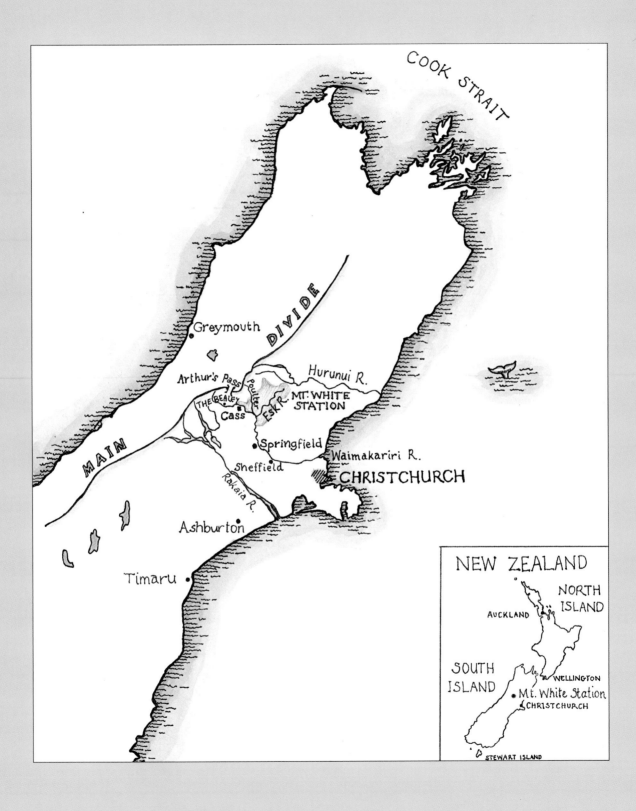

COOK STRAIT

MAIN DIVIDE

Greymouth

Arthur's Pass

Poulter

THE BEALEY

Cass

ESK R.

Hurunui R.

MT. WHITE STATION

Springfield

Waimakariri R.

CHRISTCHURCH

Sheffield

Rakaia R.

Ashburton

Timaru

NEW ZEALAND

NORTH ISLAND

AUCKLAND

SOUTH ISLAND

WELLINGTON

Mt. White Station

CHRISTCHURCH

STEWART ISLAND

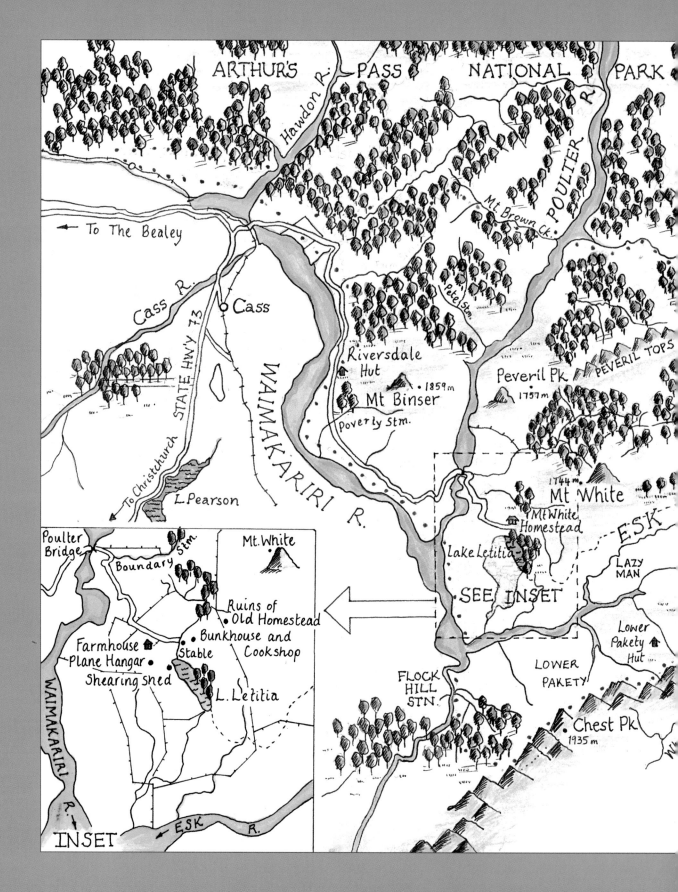

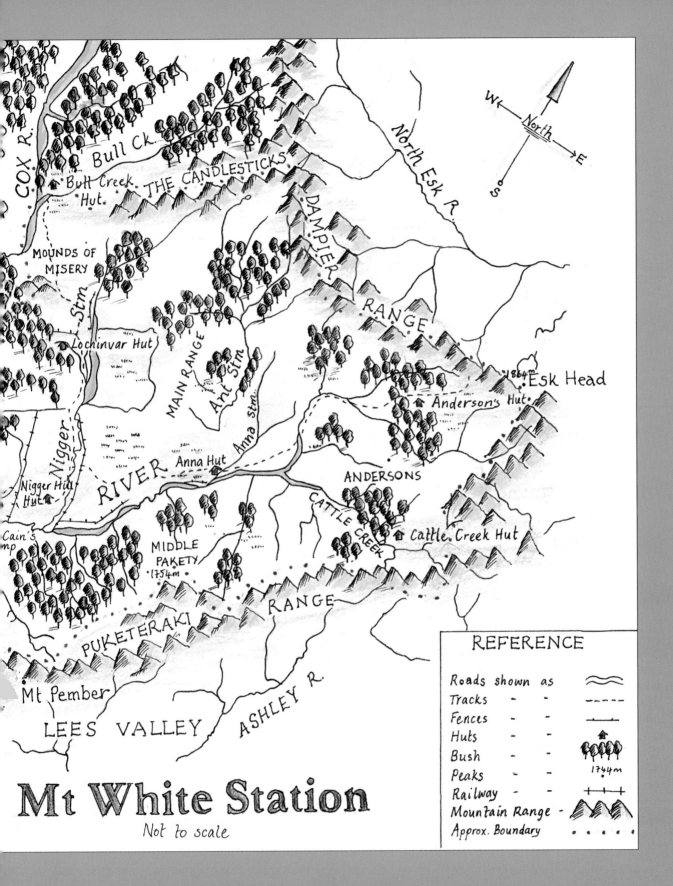

To the children of the South Island high country

CONTENTS

PREFACE 11

BOYS OF THE
HIGH COUNTRY 17
DOGS 43
MUSTERING 55
HORSES 79
CATTLE & DEER 97
SHEEP 111
FUN 123
FRIENDS 137
EVENTS 151
THE FUTURE 163

MYSTERIOUS MOUNTAIN CREATURES 168
SOME HIGH-COUNTRY TERMS 171
ACKNOWLEDGEMENTS 176

PREFACE

As an eight-year-old boy, John's favourite book — a book he read and reread almost every night — was Gay and Georg Kohlap's *David, Boy of the High Country*. This evocative book with its splendid black-and-white images took John from his inner-city Auckland home into the high country of the South Island of New Zealand, into a world so different from his own.

As he read about the lives of seven-year-old David Innes and his sister Rose, who lived on Haldon Station in the Mackenzie Country, John could hear the sheep bleating and the dogs barking. He would wonder at the vastness of the land; he would wonder what it would be like to ride a horse, to muster a mob of merinos, to see a calf born, to smell the woolshed during shearing.

A lot about farming in the high country has changed since *David, Boy of the High Country* was published in 1964, but a lot is just the same. We hope our book about Ben and Mark Smith of Mount White Station in Canterbury will enthral you as you get to know the boys and their father and mother, and discover how their life is fashioned by the cycles and seasons of farming, and by living so far away from other people, in a place where you have to make your own fun with the natural world around you.

I got to know Ben and Mark's parents, Richard and Sheri, quite soon after I moved from Auckland to Castle Hill Station, in the Upper Waimakariri Valley in Canterbury, in 2004. Richard knew Castle Hill well, as he had been the manager there before taking up the manager's job at Mount White. He was one of the first people who called in to see if I needed any help and advice running the farm. I soon learned how respected his farming skills are in the district.

My own children and grandchildren and the children in the Books In Homes programme love reading about the lives of other children. Since I have been farming I have become aware of how little knowledge New Zealanders who live in cities have of rural New Zealand. John and I both hope that this book will help city kids learn about the lives of children who live on farms, especially in the South Island high country.

Christine Fernyhough
Castle Hill Station, Canterbury
September 2009

Ben (right) and Mark in the shearing shed at Mount White Station.

This is the first gate on Ben and Mark's farm, Mount White Station. From here it will take 45 minutes to drive to their house.

BOYS
OF THE
HIGH
COUNTRY

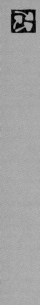

Ben and Mark Smith live on Mount White Station, right on the edge of the Southern Alps in inland Canterbury. Ben is nine and Mark is eight, and they have lived at Mount White ever since they were born. To them it is just their home, where they live with their father, Richard, who is the farm's manager, and their mother, Sheri. But if you were a visitor coming to Mount White for the very first time you would be completely amazed by the place.

It is huge — it covers 40,000 hectares. That's the same size as the whole big city of Christchurch. It's as big as nearly 60,000 rugby fields put together. Now picture those rugby fields surrounded by big mountains, with two powerful rivers, the Esk and the Poulter, rushing through from the mountains to join the mighty Waimakariri River. Their water is milky blue and icy cold, because it is fed by glaciers.

Ranges of tall mountains surround the farm. Ben and Mark are named after some of them. Ben's middle name is Puketeraki (which means 'the mountain that holds up the sky'), after the mountain range on the western edge of the station. One of Mark's middle names is Binser, after the big mountain the Smith family can see from the home paddocks near their farmhouse. These

mountains face each other, with flat land in between. On a clear day they seem to move closer and to talk to each other.

You might think that such a big place would have a grand entrance, but in fact you hardly notice the turn-off to the station, on the main road between Christchurch and Arthur's Pass, State Highway 73. Instead of keeping on going to Arthur's Pass and over to the West Coast, you turn right at a sign saying 'Mount White Bridge', and straight away you are on a narrow gravel road. It crosses over the railway line on an old white wooden bridge, then carries on through golden-coloured river flats where you might see some of Mount White's merino sheep grazing. You can't see it all when you drive in, and as the narrow gravel road goes on and on and on, you begin to realise how enormous the farm is.

The road climbs up into the hills and passes over big beds of rock and shingle that are crossed by dashing streams. It winds beneath black beech forest before bursting into the open again to show wide skies, tall, forbidding mountains and vast stretches of river flats. There are almost no fences and the land seems endless.

When you look up at the mountains in the summer, you can see that they are covered with loose shingle (or scree, as it is known), which spreads down the slopes almost like a waterfall.

Ben takes Midgee the pony for a swim in the little lake near the farmhouse. Midgee looks a bit upset but she actually really likes cooling off in the lake. ⌖

Above: Ben and Mark's father's sheep dogs Fent and Lico (short for Licorice) on the path to the lake. Right: Lines of sheep come down from the hills during a muster. ◩

You can see why these parts of New Zealand are called the high country. In the winter these slopes are covered in snow.

There are seven gates on the road between the turn-off and the farmhouse at Mount White. When Ben and Mark drive onto the farm with their mother and father, they ask themselves, "I wonder how many of the gates are open today?" If they are in the front seat they have to climb out and open and close every one of the seven gates between the road and their farmhouse.

One gate is in the middle of the bridge over the Poulter River.

Above: Ben and Mark out in the hills. Right: The main road to Mount White is narrow and winding and there are seven gates to open and close. ⬚

When the wind is howling, the gate is hard to open and the river thrashes against the rocks far below. It is very scary but also very exciting. It is Mark's favourite gate.

It is 30 kilometres from the main road to their house. Ben and Mark are used to it, but visitors always say they can't believe how far away their house is from the road.

The farmhouse is only a third of the way into the station. There's even more land way out the back. During the two big sheep musters at Mount White each year, in October and April, the musterers who round up the sheep go out for seven nights and move between a series of huts, where they sleep each night. One of those huts is 45 kilometres from the farmhouse.

Ben and Mark's father has been the manager of the station for seventeen years. He is a very experienced farmer who is widely respected throughout the Upper Waimakariri Valley, which is what local people call the district. When Ben and Mark's father left school, he got a job on a farm in Southland and by the time he was eighteen he had his first working sheep dog. His first job

On the way to the farmhouse, Mark throws a rock off the Poulter Bridge into the water below.

a manager was on Castle Hill Station, further down the valley. He was only twenty-seven years old when he became the manager at Mount White. That is very young to have such a big job, being in charge of thirteen thousand sheep and eleven hundred valuable cattle and deer.

He met Ben and Mark's mother, Sheri, when she came to his brother's wedding. A few years after they married Ben and Mark came along, and when they did their parents were thrilled, as they had looked forward to having children who would love the station as much as they did and who could learn all about farming from them. Like all high-country people, Ben and Mark's parents work very hard, every day of the week, and they know how to cope with all sorts of tough conditions.

Left: Ben and Mark and their father come back from a day out hunting. Ben is carrying a dead wild pig on his shoulders. If pigs aren't hunted there will be too many of them and they will damage the pasture. Above: Ben and Mark's father and mother, Richard and Sheri. ⊠

Mount White is a very famous station. It dates back to the mid-1850s and has always been one of the largest stations in the South Island. There have been many books written about it.

Ben and Mark live in the new Mount White farmhouse. The original farmhouse was pulled down about ten years ago and it was then over a hundred years old. Ben and Mark sometimes go up to look at where it stood. They can see the concrete foundations

and the remains of the limestone chimney, and there are rusty, square-headed nails lying everywhere. It always seems odd to the boys how the old taps still stick up out of the concrete on their copper pipes. Their father has a joke that the last family to live in the house had to leave it because the plumbing was no good.

Nearby there is a rusted-out crankshaft still attached to a water wheel. It was used to drive a chaff cutter, which cut up oats to make food for the horses. The old orchard is now just a row of gnarled trees but a crab-apple and an apple tree still have fruit.

A little way off from where the old house used to stand is a small headstone which reads, 'In memory of Minnie Cochran, October 27 1874. Baby.' She must have been the daughter of the farm manager at that time, and it makes Ben and Mark a bit sad

Ben and Mark sometimes play around the ruins of the old farmhouse, where there's a grave and an old water wheel.

when they think about her being buried in the ground beneath their feet.

Not far away are the shearers' quarters, a row of bunkrooms opening onto a wooden veranda. This building is where the shearers and other farm workers sleep. It is also over a hundred years old.

The people who have worked on Mount White over the years love the station, and the knowledge of all its managers has been passed down from generation to generation. In the dining room at the farmhouse there are shelves of managers' diaries, one for every year going right back to 1925.

Farmers in other areas know how sturdy and well-bred Mount White's sheep, cattle and deer are, and they are always keen to buy animals from the station when they come up for sale.

🌀

It is not easy to live on a station like Mount White. It is very beautiful but it is also very tough country.

In spring the station seems to burst into life as the sun warms the soil and rain showers make new, sweet grass grow. The paddocks are full of lambs and calves and fawns.

But then summer comes, and it gets hot and dry. Sometimes it gets too dry. Ben and Mark's parents are always relieved when the rain comes and the grass can start growing again.

In winter it is extremely cold and there is lots of deep snow. The snow comes down around the house and sometimes

The apple tree at the old farmhouse orchard still has fruit but the apples are really sour. 🌀

Washing day at the bunkhouse, where the shearers and farm workers sleep.

blocks the road so no one can get in or out. Sometimes the snow comes as early as April and the family needs lots of firewood to keep the wood stove going to heat the house all through the long, cold winters. If the snow brings the power lines down, the family has to cook on the kerosene Aga, and use candles for lighting.

Because the station is so isolated, Sheri has to be very organised to make sure there is always enough food in the freezer. If she needs something for cooking, she can't just go down to the shop. The nearest town is Springfield, and it takes an hour and a half to get there from the farmhouse. She grows vegetables (she's famous for her rhubarb), looks after the hens that give the family their eggs, and keeps beehives for honey.

The family gets all its eggs from its own hens. They're soft to hold, until they decide to escape from your hands. ▣

If someone has an accident, or if any people or animals get sick or into trouble, it is a long way to go for help. Once Sheri got a flat tyre on the farm road and had to walk 17 kilometres back to the house. It's too far for an ambulance to come if someone needs to go to hospital. Ben and Mark can still remember the day the rescue helicopter flew in to pick up their friend Murray Harford, who had broken his collarbone.

But Ben and Mark don't ever think about the tough things about life on Mount White. To them it is a wonderful place to live. They have a small motorbike of their own that they double up on. They have horses to ride and creeks to play in. They have their own sheep dogs and a lake to swim in and they are learning more and more about farming every year.

Ben and Mark used to get their lessons from The Correspondence School, which is a very famous schooling system for children who live in isolated places. Every fortnight, they would receive lessons sent out from the school in Wellington, and would go through them with their parents. The schoolwork was sent back to Wellington for marking and comments, and once a term a visiting teacher would call in at the station. Then two years ago, The Correspondence School told Ben and Mark's parents that the visiting teacher would not be able to come any more to help them. The boys had been enjoying doing the lessons with their mother

Sheri keeps beehives and makes her own honey. She is checking a hive wearing her protective gear. ▣

but they would have to start going to a normal school.

The nearest primary school is in Springfield and there isn't a school bus, so Sheri would have to drive for several hours every day to take the boys to school and back. The family decided that the best thing would be for Sheri and the boys to live in Springfield during the week and come home on the weekends.

So every Monday, Sheri and Ben and Mark get in the four-wheel-drive at seven o'clock and set out on the long drive to Springfield. They drive back again on Friday afternoons after school. In winter it is a very hard drive as they have to come over Porters Pass, which is a very steep and winding road that can be slippery with ice. It is almost dark by the time they start on the road to the station.

Springfield lies far away from Mount White on the other side of the Puketeraki Range. During the week, Ben and Mark's father can look at the sky beyond the 'Paketys', as the mountains are called. He can tell what the weather is like where Ben and Mark are and imagine what they might be doing.

Ben and Mark miss their father very much during the week. It's better in winter, when he drives down in the middle of the week to coach their rugby team and stays with them overnight. They enjoy being in Springfield, where there are a lot more people and friends who come and play every day after school. But when they are all back together at the farmhouse on Friday evening, the boys know that they also love the space and freedom of being on Mount White. It is the best place of all.

Mark's father helps him onto Midgee's back. ◪

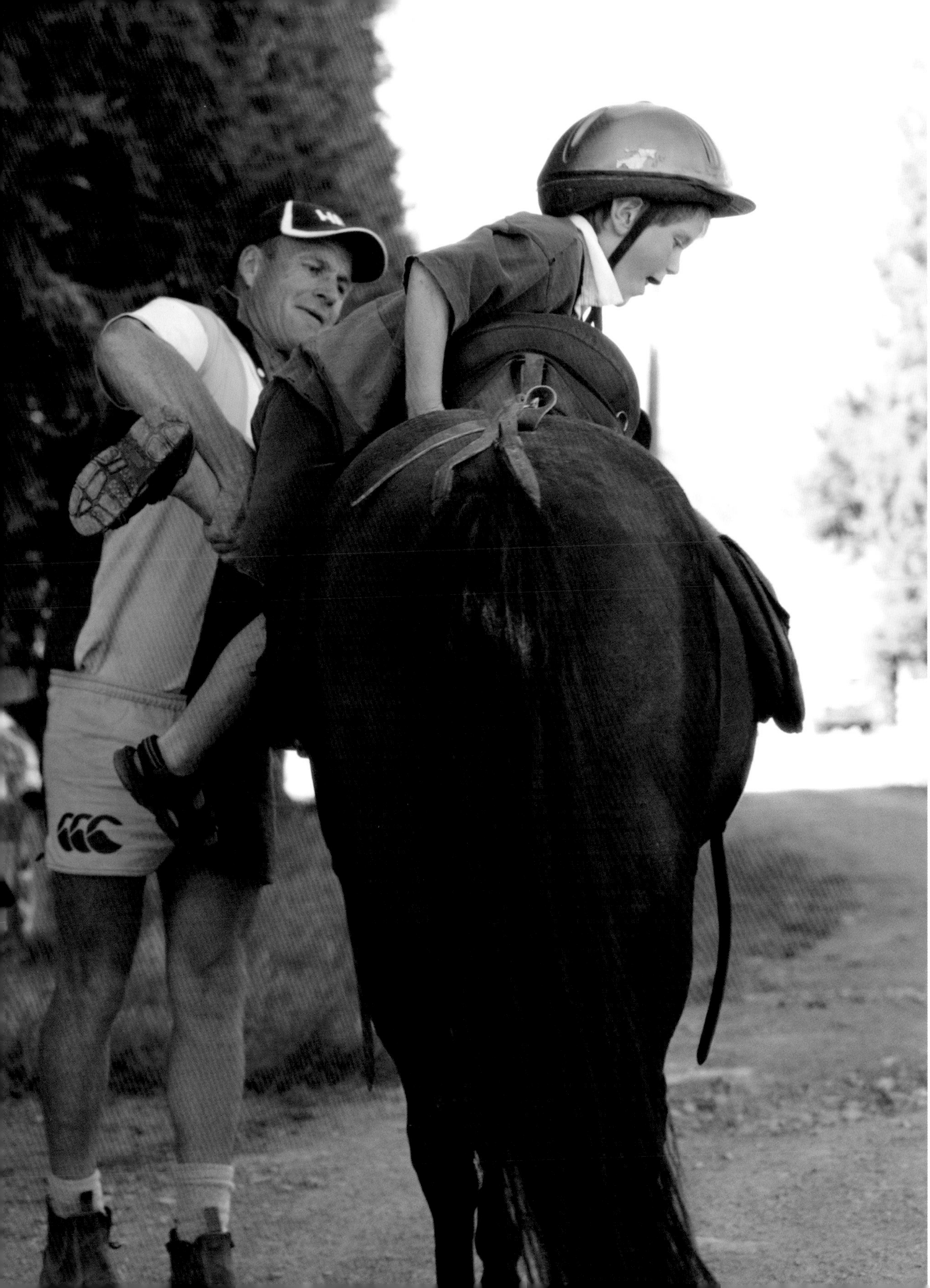

DOGS

Sheep dogs are Mount White's real workers, and it would be impossible to farm the station without them. These days four-wheel-drives, which farmers call their 'trucks', can pick their way around steep slopes and across rivers, but they can't get right into the far back country and up the really high slopes where merinos love to graze. The rugged high country is a place for a farmer on foot or on horseback, and his team of dogs is always with him.

Farmers have used dogs ever since farming began in New Zealand and it is amazing to watch them working together. It is an incredible partnership. The dogs have been trained to respond to whistles or special calls, and they can bring a flock of sheep down off the hills simply by listening to their owner's commands, even if the farmer is standing a long, long way away from them.

One of most important jobs on a high-country farm is mustering the animals. Just as in the old days, every musterer has a team of dogs. There are two kinds of sheep dog, each with a special role to play. Eye dogs, or heading dogs, herd the sheep by staring at them rather than barking at them. They are Border collies, a breed which comes from the border between England and Scotland.

The other sort of dog is called a huntaway. These are large dogs, often black and tan in colour. Huntaways are trained to drive the sheep forward by barking behind them. Sometimes farmers also have what is called a handy dog, which can both 'head' and 'hunt'.

Ben and Mark's father has six dogs in his team, one heading

Mark decides to teach Fent a few new tricks. ⊠

dog and five huntaways. He always has other new dogs he is training up and some which have retired from daily work.

After eight or nine years of working hard, sheep dogs get footsore and tired. They can't keep up with the spirited sheep and cows anymore, so they live out their days around the farmhouse. Ben and Mark's family has an old dog called Speights. She looks a bit like those old musterers, all grey and whiskery. She got her funny name, Ben and Mark's father says, because she arrived at the station as a little puppy in a Speight's beer carton.

Speights is often found around the back door with Migsee, the family's Jack Russell terrier. Migsee is two years old and Ben and Mark's father says he punches above his weight, sometimes taking on large huntaways which are three times his size. Migsee's favourite place is in Ben and Mark's father's truck, behind the headrest on the driver's side, where he looks as if he is giving instructions.

Ben and Mark are keen to get their own teams of dogs. They already have one each. Ben has Zac, a handy dog given to him by Kieran Rowlands, who sometimes musters on Mount White. Mark's dog Shy is a

Left: Ben and Mark's father's dogs have their own travelling box on the back of his truck. Above: Migsee in his favourite place in the truck. ⊠

heading dog and she was given to him by Dave Prebble, who also helps to muster on the station. The boys have their own dog whistles and their father has started to help them train their dogs. Shy already eyes up the hens that peck around the shrubs in the garden.

The boys have favourites in their father's team of dogs, too. They like Fent because he is clever, and they also like Podge. He is the biggest dog on the farm and is so tough he can catch wild pigs.

Above: Migsee and Speights look a bit worried. Speights has her front legs crossed, which farmers say is a sign of intelligence in a working dog. Right: Mark's dog Shy is learning to be working dog. She's decided to start by rounding up the hens. ⊠

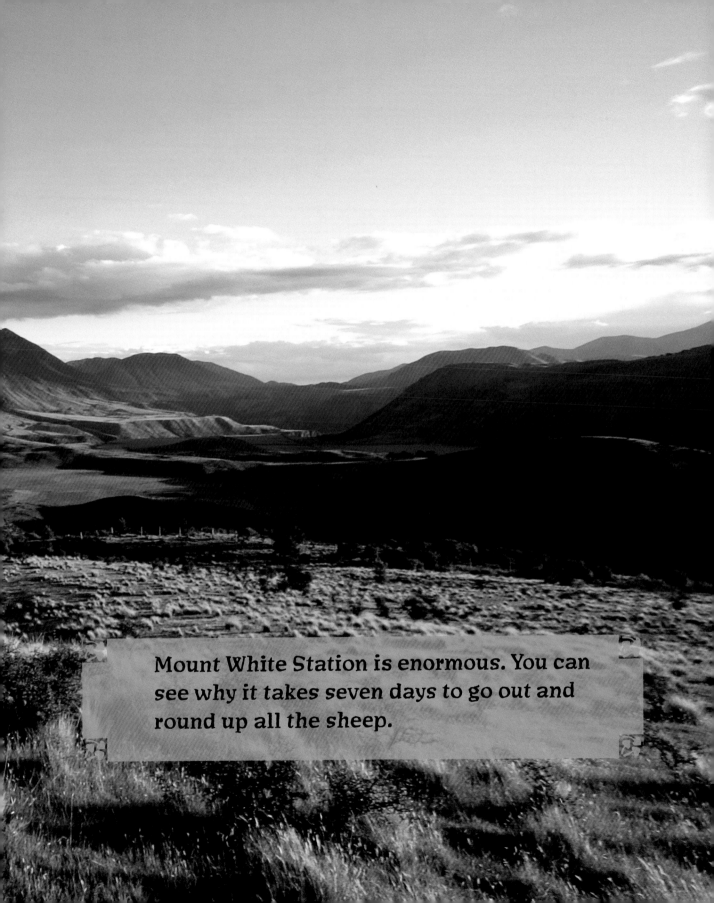

Mount White Station is enormous. You can see why it takes seven days to go out and round up all the sheep.

MUSTERING

Over the past hundred and fifty years, hundreds of musterers have worked on Mount White. The first shepherds came from Scotland in the 1860s. When Ben and Mark look at photos from the old days they can see that these men wore bulky, scratchy woollen clothes, felt hats and heavy boots with hobnails, that gave them grip on slippery ground. It couldn't have been very comfortable.

The shepherds are also known as musterers, when they get together in groups to bring sheep down from the hills onto the flats for shearing. Some come back year after year to be part of the station's twice-yearly musters. On the sideboard in the farmhouse there is a photo of a Mount White musterers' reunion in 1992. Some of the really old men in the photo walked what is called the 'top beat', high up in the hills, way back in the 1930s.

When Ben and Mark are older they will start going out for all the big spring and autumn musters with their father and all the other musterers to bring the sheep down from the hills. After the spring muster the sheep are shorn and sent back up to the high country for the summer. The autumn muster brings the stock down from the summer country to the winter paddocks on the

Riversdale flats, where they can be looked after. Because in winter there is no fresh grass for the sheep to eat, Ben and Mark 's father and his workers will 'feed out' silage (a sort of fermented grass which sheep find delicious). Sometimes it is so cold or there is so much snow on the ground that there is no new grass for over four months. It is really important that lots of silage is made in the summer and stored over autumn.

When Ben and Mark go on their first sheep muster they will become part of the mustering heritage of Mount White. They will walk and ride into the beautiful high country. They will see high,

Geoff Rowlands is one of the regular musterers at Mount White Station. He's riding Bob, the station's 'bomb-proof' horse.

MUSTERING 58

high mountains, snow tussocks, scree slopes, rich green valleys and magical places like little Lake Grace, hidden among the mountains.

They will stay the night in one of the station's six huts: Lower Pakety, Anna, Nigger, Riversdale, Cattle Creek and Cain's Camp. Some of these huts are more than a hundred years old. Over the years musterers have carved their names and even short sayings into the walls.

The old Cattle Creek hut is made from the trunks of beech trees cut from the nearby bush. It is clad with corrugated iron

Migsee stands guard on the top of the silage pit. The tyres keep the plastic from blowing off. ⊠

and inside there are old pots and pans and billies, battered from decades of use. The fireplace is thick with ash and tea towels are hung on a string above the fire. A huge square of limestone rock hangs from the rafters, holding the roof down so it does not blow off in big storms.

When the musterers get to one of these huts, the 'packie' will be waiting for them. It's his job to look after the musterers. He will have brought in all the sleeping and cooking gear and all the food, and will have the dinner on.

People using the old huts often carve their names in the timber.

Ben and Mark will be really tired from working all day and after dinner they will soon be asleep on the bunks. In the morning, like all those musterers before them, they will complain about someone snoring in the night.

Once out on the tops the next day, they will learn why the old-timers call a steep climb a 'pipe-opener': it opens up your windpipe and makes you puff! At dinner each night they will listen to all the tall tales and the stories of tricky jobs well done. On every muster something new or different happens that

The old Nigger Hut, which is now used to store saddles and firewood, is over a hundred years old. ⊠

Inside the Cattle Creek Hut. It hasn't changed much since it was built in 1945. It's the farthest away from the farmhouse and a favourite because it has not been modernised and all the cooking is still done on the fire.

becomes a story in its own right.

The boys will be given their own place on what is called a beat. The musterers on the top beat head out first, sometimes as early as four in the morning, and walk and ride as far as they can up the highest ridges and peaks. Their huntaway dogs will bark as they go, flushing the sheep out of the tussocks and thorny matagouri bushes and off rocky outcrops. Then the musterers use the dogs to send the sheep they have rounded up down to the lower beats. The next set of musterers adds the sheep they have rounded up to the mob and keep moving it down the hill.

The mob of sheep gets bigger as it comes down the hills. From the valley floor the sheep look like tiny white ants or salt, pouring down the hills. The mob is led by the older sheep that always

Left: Mark, his father and his father's dogs Fent, Podge and Lico have a short rest during a muster.

seem to know the way to go.

By the time they get to the yards there will be around thirteen thousand of them. It is quite a scene: the noise of the sheep bleating, the dogs barking, the musterers using their 'special language' as Ben and Mark's father calls it (they think he really means swearing), the dust in the air and that special sheep smell that high-country farmers know so well.

A stray lamb or two is often brought in lying across a musterer's saddle, waiting to join its mother at the yards. It's incredible that a young lamb and its mother can find each other in such a crowd, but they do.

The sheep race around a steep corner on their way to the shearing shed to have their wool clipped off.

Like their father and the musterers of old, Ben and Mark will learn
to read the sky and understand what the clouds, the mist, the
wind and the changing temperatures tell them about the coming
weather. If it rains, the rivers will rise and become too dangerous
to cross. The muster will have to stop until the water level drops.

Ben and Mark will both need a trusty hill stick or mustering
stick. It is a tradition for musterers to go into the bush and select

The mustering gang arrives back at the cookhouse and
the gear is piled up on the porch. ⚐

their own stick from a young, straight manuka tree. It is then cut to size, and the bark is rubbed off with the blade of a hunting knife. The sticks become smooth and dark with use. Ben and Mark will use them for keeping their balance when walking on scree slopes, for stability when crossing creeks and rivers, to test boggy ground where a horse may become caught, and for giving their horses a gentle tap on the rump to get them to move forward. They will learn to use them as an extension of their arms when giving instructions to their dogs. They will treasure their sticks and will keep them for years. They will not leave home without them.

Above: Mark leans on his hill stick as he watches the hundreds of sheep streaming through the valley. ⌖

Ben and Mark will also come to know what it is like to be really exhausted. Days in the open, travelling over rocky ground for hours, are long and hard. They will sometimes work in the searing heat of the sun and at other times in freezing temperatures, made even colder by the chill wind blowing at their backs. They will start work in the cool mornings wearing several layers of clothes and take one off at a time as the day warms up. By the end of the day they may have to put them all back on again as the temperatures drop. People say that in the high country you can have four seasons in one day.

A day's mustering is such hard work that it is a relief when someone calls for smoko. A fire is lit at the hut, the billy is filled with water from the river and the tea leaves are tipped in. When the water has boiled, a musterer pours the tea into everyone's enamel mugs. They all take sugar because everyone needs the energy. The big sandwiches never taste better.

In the old days, the men would then bring out their pipes or tobacco pouches and cigarette papers to roll their

Above: Musterer Ben Booth and his dogs. Right: Towards the end of the muster Mark and his father get a ride while the dogs run behind. Fent is the lucky one who gets to sit on the back with them. ▨

The end of the muster is in sight as the mob of sheep heads through the last set of gates.

own cigarettes, which is why this break is called smoko. But Ben and Mark, like their father, are never going to smoke.

Right at the very end of the muster, after days of hard work, everyone gets together in the cookhouse for a big meal, with beer

Above: Ben with his Grandpa George (right), Kieran Rowlands (left) and Mark Sampson the packie outside the cookhouse at the end of the muster. Mark has done more than fifty musters on Mount White over twenty-five years. Right: Inside the cookhouse everyone tucks in to a big lunch. ⊠

to wash it down. Everyone has sore bottoms from riding and aching feet from walking. They talk of what the dogs did wrong and right, and there are lots of jokes and teasing and laughter. When Mark gets tired of listening he goes into the games room next door to throw darts. His father jokes that every now and then a dart flies into the dining room, nearly hitting the gang sitting around the table.

Left: Mark's darts sometimes go flying into the dining room next door. Above: Some of the mustering crew relax outside the cookhouse at the end of a long day. ⊠

HORSES

Next to dogs, horses are the most important working animals on a high-country station like Mount White. These days many farmers use quad bikes and motorbikes and their four-wheel-drive trucks to round up sheep. Sometimes they even use helicopters. But at Mount White, mustering is still done the old way because horseback is the only way to reach into the far back country.

There are usually about twenty horses, which are called station hacks, on the property. Ben and Mark's father is always breeding new ones. Most of the hacks are part-Clydesdale, which is a breed of draught horse, and they are very sturdy, with shaggy soft coats and great big hooves that make them very sure-footed on the uneven ground.

Ben and Mark's father knows a lot about horses. When he was just twelve years old he worked before and after school at a racing stable outside Timaru. He is teaching the boys how to ride and how to work the horses with cattle and sheep. The horses need to be very calm so they won't upset the stock. They are very good at turning sharply and they can pick their way carefully across rocky ground, so all their riders have to do is look out for the cattle and sheep.

Ben and Mark's father has a horse called Nike, who has a big white mark on his forehead that looks like the Nike tick. Their favourite is Bob, a huge black horse with a noble head and deep, dark brown eyes. They love the way he feels. His coat is so soft. He is seventeen hands high (or 1.7 metres) at his shoulder, and when they are sitting on his back it feels as if they are on a big moving ship. But they are never frightened being up so high because Bob is so gentle and calm. Ben and Mark's father says he is bomb-proof.

At Mount White, the stables are near the cookhouse. This is where everyone keeps their saddles and bridles and halters. After a day out mustering, the horses are brushed down by their riders to remove all the sweat that has built up on their coats, especially under the saddle.

Left and above left: Ben and Mark's friend Geoff Rowlands with Bob, the biggest horse on Mount White Station. Above right: Back at the stables, Mark talks softly to Bob.

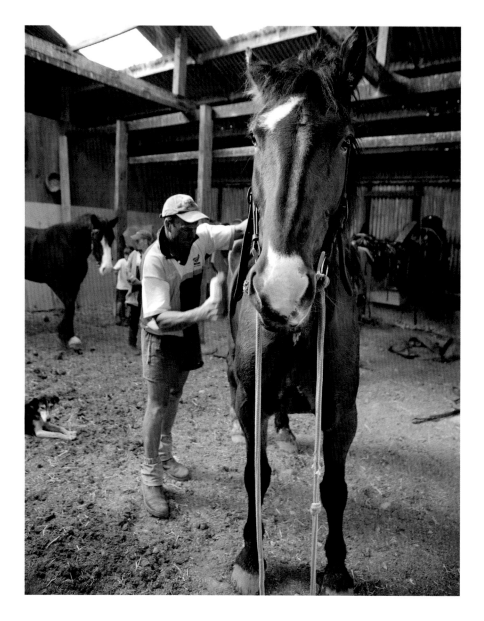

Above: Ben and Mark's father brushes down his horse
Nike after a hard day's riding. Right: Mark holds the
reins of Little Black Horse while he waits for someone
to take off her saddle. ⊠

HORSES 84

The horses get new shoes every six weeks, so their hooves don't get damaged by the rough ground. Rather than a blacksmith coming to the station, Ben and Mark's father does most of the shoeing himself. He also teaches the musterers to shoe their own horses.

First he heats up the metal horseshoes, then he nails them onto the horses' hooves. Then he uses a rasp to file back the hooves so that they fit exactly under the shoe. It's like filing a person's fingernails. It doesn't hurt the horses at all.

When they are not being ridden, the horses hang around in the paddock together. As well as Nike and Bob, there are Sue and Poppy and Jimmy and Joe. The Little Black Horse got her name because she is so small. She was accidentally separated from her mother when she was little and has never grown up as big as the other draught horses.

Ben's favourite is Poppy, who is grey, and Mark likes riding the little pony called Midgee, which is short for Midget. She was lent to him by a family friend, Heather Harrington, who is a horse trekker. Mark loves to throw his arms around Midgee's neck and press his face into her mane.

Ben and Mark already do quite a lot of riding. For the last

Ben and Mark's father shoes all the horses on Mount White. Rusty old worn-out shoes gather cobwebs on the stable wall. ⌖

Ben and Mark walk out to see the horses. Bob, in the centre, has huge hooves.

three Christmases they have gone camping on Flock Hill, the neighbouring station. They camp with their friends the Hills, who manage the station, and the Gunns, who live on Brooksdale Station further down the valley.

One year they rode out to the camping site with their mother and they had to cross the river. It was running a bit high and Sheri was worried that it was too deep and dangerous to cross. She put Mark up on her horse and let Midgee swim across on her own. The little pony almost got swept away in the fast-moving water but she is such a determined little horse that she eventually got to the safety of the bank on the other side.

Mark carries the bridle out to Midgee, then leads her back to have her saddle put on. ⌘

Ben and Mark were excited when one of the Mount White mares, named Brew after a racehorse that won the Melbourne Cup, had a foal. They named her Viewed after another Melbourne Cup winner. Her father was a horse from Erewhon Station, which is famous for its big, strong horses.

Straight after the foal was born, Ben and Mark's father started to handle her. He told them it is important to do this often, touching every single part of the foal's body in the first three days of its life, so it gets used to being handled by people and can later on be broken in or trained. This is called imprinting.

Ben and Mark went to see the foal each day with their father. He got the foal to lie down so he could touch her feet to prepare her for the day when she would have the first horseshoes put on her hooves.

The foal was so relaxed being with Ben and Mark and their father that she lay with her head in Mark's lap, just like an oversized dog. She is going to be kept to work on the station and Ben and Mark are looking forward to seeing her grow up.

Ben, Mark and their father get the new foal used to people by touching her all over.

A bend in the Poulter River in the middle of Mount White Station. The big mountain in the middle of this photo is Mount White itself.

CATTLE & DEER

M ount White Station usually has around six hundred cattle. They are Herefords, which are brown cattle with white splotches, a breed which is ideal for high-country conditions. They can cope with the rough land and the hot summers and cold winters.

These cattle are bred for their meat only — it is too dry and there is not enough grass for dairy cows on Mount White. In the old days there were always a couple of milking cows on the property to supply the manager's family and all the workers with milk. A man was employed to look after the cows and also the vegetable garden. He was known as the 'cow man gardener'. Today all the milk that Ben and Mark drink comes in a big crate from the shop in Springfield and is kept in the freezer.

It is always exciting in spring when calving begins. Ben and Mark are sometimes lucky enough to see calves being born and watch them get up on their wobbly legs and take their first drink from their mothers. The mother cows are very protective of their calves, and you have to be careful not to get too close to them or they will charge at you. In fact, both Ben and Mark have been knocked down by calves. Neither of them was badly hurt but they

are a bit more wary of cows now.

Sometimes there are some very sad stories during the calving season. One day Mark was out with his father in the truck when they found a calf almost drowned in the creek. Only her head was sticking out of the water. It was only about four days old and its mother was nowhere to be seen. Something bad must have happened to her because cows are always very good mothers. They found out later that the mother cow had died.

Ben and Mark's father managed to get the calf out of the creek and onto the back of the truck, then they quickly drove back to the house. The poor little calf was very ill so Ben and Mark's mother made up some calf formula and put it into a bottle with a big rubber teat. The calf sucked away hungrily and soon it seemed to be much better. They kept it close to the house for about three more days.

It was a pretty little calf and the boys grew very fond of it. But then one morning they found it had died in the night. The family was really sad about it. Ben and Mark's mother says, 'She was such a trier.' That same year, however, Sheri hand-reared three more orphaned calves that all survived and were able to go back into the paddock with the rest of the herd.

There are often sad stories about animals on a big station like Mount White. The old-timers say, 'Where there's livestock, there's dead stock.' The boys have got used to the fact that sometimes some animals get unwell or have accidents but they still feel sad when an animal they have become fond of dies.

Ben and Mark's mother, Sheri, with the little calf she tried to save by hand-feeding it from a milk bottle. ⊠

All children like to have their own money but it's hard to earn it when you live so far away from a town where you might get a job. So one day when he was at the cattle sales, Ben and Mark's father had a bright idea. He decided to keep four of the steers he had planned to sell and to give two each to Ben and Mark. They liked this idea and gave him all their saved-up pocket money to buy the steers. It is going to be their job to look after them and make sure they grow fat and strong. When the steers are older, Ben and Mark can sell them and put the money into their own savings accounts at the bank.

At the end of the cattle muster, the cows and calves run into the cattle yards.

There are two cattle musters every year on Mount White, and Ben has already been on his first one. It was a great adventure for him and he rode Bob a lot of the way. When he talked about it in a speech competition at school he won a prize, and later the speech was printed on the front page of the local newspaper.

The autumn muster is in April. The musterers bring the cattle down from the high country to graze on the lower paddocks, where they will stay for the winter and be looked after when the snow falls. Unlike the sheep, the tough old cattle always manage to find something to eat on their own.

The cattle stir up clouds of dust as they run past Ben and Mark's father, who is counting them.

Their thick coats will keep them warm in the freezing temperatures. When it gets really cold, they huddle together to keep warm or push into bushes and scrub for shelter.

In the December muster, the new calves which have been born in springtime are brought in to be ear-tagged. All stock on New Zealand farms have to be tagged with a number which identifies the farm the animals have come from. This way it is easy to trace any animals which might have a serious disease such as tuberculosis or foot-and-mouth disease.

After this the calves are weaned — separated from their mothers so they don't rely on them for milk anymore and start eating only grass. Most of them are then sold, except for any female calves that Ben and Mark's father plans to keep with the herd to replace some of the older cows. They will have their own calves the next year, after they have been mated with a bull. The bulls are put into the same paddock as the cows for a few weeks and then the cows are pregnant for about nine months — the same time as a human.

Left: With the cattle shut in the yards, Ben and Mark ask their father and Murray Harford questions about the stock. This is how they learn about farming. ⊠

After the last muster, Ben and Mark had the job of counting the herd as they ran through the gate out of the cattle yards. They got a bit mixed up and ended up counting twice as many as there really were, so their father had to do it all over again.

When it was all done, the grown-ups stood around talking in the yards. Sometimes it can get a bit boring listening to them talk, but Ben and Mark's father says the best farming decisions are always made in the yard.

❧

At the end of their farming lesson Murray teases Mark by poking him with his stick. ❧

Mount White has a big herd of red deer, too. Like most high-country farms, Mount White is a breeding farm only, because there is not enough grass for the deer to eat to grow to a good size. They sell the young deer (known as weaners) to farmers in lowland areas. Lowland farms get plenty of rainfall and sunshine so the grass continues to grow all the year round, except for a few weeks in midwinter, and the deer can grow big and strong.

In early autumn, when the deer are on one of the big paddocks close to the farmhouse, the family will often drive out to check on them. As the truck approaches, the deer lift their heads and the herd starts to move. They run swiftly and elegantly, and the herd looks like a torrent of red-brown liquid as it moves. The mother deer, which are called hinds, keep the little fawns with their spotted coats close alongside.

When their father stops the truck and switches off the engine, Ben and Mark can hear the deer 'talking' — a noise like thousands of women clicking along in high stiletto heels or gossiping to each other. It's an amazing sound: hundreds and hundreds of clicks and whinnies.

Most of the five hundred deer at Mount White are hinds, but there are also thirty stags, or male deer. These stags have massive antlers, which are rough like coral, and so heavy that it is hard to imagine a deer could hold up his head with such a weight. Every spring each stag's set of antlers either falls off naturally or is cut off by Ben and Mark's father, then a new set starts to grow. The growth for the first three months is called velvet, because it is much softer than the fully grown antlers and is covered in a soft fuzz. After that stage it keeps growing into a new, huge set of antlers, each year bigger than the last.

On the garage wall near the house Ben and Mark's father has hung up some of the discarded sets of antlers. He has explained to the boys how the stags use their antlers. It's very clever. When the stags lower their heads to fight with each other, the points on them become stabbing weapons. But when they run through trees they lift their heads up and tilt them back slightly so that the antlers point backwards and don't get tangled in the branches.

You can never really tame a deer, even when they have been bred on a farm. They are not as easy to manage as sheep or cattle and they have to be looked after in a special way because they are easily startled or upset. They have to have specially designed deer yards. The animals come into the Mount White deer shed through a series of long, narrow chutes, and the further into the shed they go the darker it becomes. This is designed to keep them calm.

Dogs are never allowed in the deer or cattle yards as the animals have to be moved carefully and quietly. Any sudden movement, such as a dog running, can upset them and because they are such big, strong animals, if they kick or rear up someone could get hurt.

Ben and Mark's father is a careful teacher and makes sure he tells the boys all about livestock, so they can benefit from his years of experience. They are learning so much, it won't be many years before they are as expert as he is.

Ben and Mark play with the sets of huge deer antlers that hang on the garage wall. ⌧

SHEEP

The New Zealand high country is famous for a very special breed of sheep known as the merino. They are easy to muster because they like to stick together rather than running off and causing the musterers and their dogs lots of problems, and they can cope with the tough climate. They also have very beautiful, fine wool.

Merino is the most valued and highly priced sheep wool in the world. It can be woven or knitted into all sorts of things: suits, jerseys, underwear, socks, blankets, shawls and rugs.

Unlike the breeds of sheep that live on lowland farms and need lots of lush grass, merinos don't mind the fact that there is not very much grass to eat on the dry, steep high-country hills. They can live, as the saying goes, 'on the smell of an oily rag'.

One good thing about living in the high country is that the merinos have very healthy feet. They love to scrape their hooves on the rocky scree slopes. This prevents them from getting a disease called foot rot, which is caused by a bacteria that lives in cracks and crevices in sheep's hooves. Sheep with foot rot can't move around to find food for themselves and their lambs.

In September each year the three thousand merino ewes, or female sheep, that live on Mount White are mustered and taken to

the shearing shed for their annual shear. The shearing is done by a group, or gang, of shearers, who stay at Mount White for several days while the shearing is done and then move on to the next farm that needs them.

The ewes are shorn of their precious wool at this time of the year so they will not get too hot over the summer months. Even though it is spring it can still be quite cold, so the shearers are careful to leave enough wool on each sheep so it can survive if temperatures drop or there is a late snowfall.

Left: These merinos have just had the shaggy wool on their foreheads trimmed back so they can see better. It's called having an eyewig. Above: In the shearing shed Ben holds onto the hoist that lifts the wool bales up into a loft to be loaded onto a truck and taken to be sold.

Above: The merinos wait outside the shearing shed for their turn to be shorn. Right: Inside, Mark watches as the shearers carefully clip off the precious wool. The rouseabout is sweeping the shorn wool into piles.

The wethers, or male sheep that are not able to breed, are shorn a little later, in October. Mount White has nine thousand wethers and it takes a whole week to shear them all — longer if it has been raining and their wool has got wet.

Before Christmas, and sometimes after, the ewes and their lambs are mustered again to one of the four tailing yards on the station. The lambs are ear-marked and a small rubber band is put around their tails, which will make them fall off about a month later. This is done because if tails are left on, their backsides will become dirty with hard, dry droppings, or dags, and this can cause disease. Taking off their tails helps to keep the sheep healthy.

The male lambs are castrated, which means they won't be able to breed. From then on they are known as wethers.

In February the ewes are mustered again. The lambs are taken from their mothers, which is called weaning. Some lambs are sold to other farmers, some females will be kept to replace the older ewes in the flock, and most of the male lambs are kept for their wool.

All the sheep are then crutched — the wool around their backsides is clipped to remove any dags hanging around which might encourage disease. The sheep are also dipped — sprayed with a chemical that gives them protection from a serious problem called fly strike.

The shearing has finished for another year and the shearers have moved on to the next farm. After seven busy days, all is quiet in the shed.

The Waimakariri River starts up in the
mountains behind Mount White Station and
flows out onto the Canterbury Plains on its
way to the sea. It forms the southern boundary
of the station. The land to the left of the river
belongs to Flock Hill and Craigieburn stations.
The big mountain on the right is Mount Binser.
Mark's middle name is Binser.

FUN

There are many places to explore and lots of fun things to do on Mount White Station, and you don't have to go very far from the farmhouse to find them.

Not every family has its own lake to swim in but Ben and Mark do. Not far from the house is a beautiful lake called Lake Letitia. Ben and Mark's father has told them that it was named after the wife of one of the station's first owners. At one end it is fringed by tall raupo reeds. A narrow grass track leads to a small jetty where there is a kayak and a white dinghy. Ben and Mark can clip on the two-horsepower Seagull motor and take the dinghy out on the water. They wish it could go a bit faster than it does.

There is also a diving board made of a thick piece of wood, which bounces on an old truck spring.

The water is very clear and cold and the lake is very deep in the middle — about 16 metres to the bottom. Ben and Mark have snorkels and goggles and they love using them when they swim at the lake.

When Ben and Mark's Grandpa George comes over from Australia, he takes the boys fishing. He shows them how to fish for trout, and he tells them stories of the time he caught the biggest rainbow trout the lake could hold. 'It was a world record,' he says.

Ben and Mark love to go out at night with spears and spotlights to catch eels. Sonny Hodgson, who works for their father on the station, sometimes cooks the eels for them.

As Ben and Mark have got better at riding they have been able to take their horses out into the lake. They stay on their backs while the horses have a swim. It is a lovely thing for the boys and the horses to do on a really hot summer's day at Mount White.

Ben and Mark also share a small motorbike. The boys put on their big helmets and take off around the paddocks. They are both really good drivers, as their father has been letting them sit on his knee to steer the farm truck and the tractor, which they call Ernie, since they were little boys. They love riding their motorbike but they love riding the horses more.

They have bicycles, too. There is no tarseal at Mount White so the boys had to learn to ride on rough paddocks and stony ground, which is a bit scary when you know you might fall off.

Close to the house there is a little creek called Boundary Creek, which Ben and Mark like to dam up with big river stones.

On a hot day the boys like to take their horses for swim in the lake. Ben goes in first on Midgee and then Mark follows. Their father is on his horse, Bob, keeping a watchful eye. ⊠

FUN 127

Sometimes they try to catch tadpoles and cockabullies, which are little native fish. They don't have any scales so they are really slippery and hard to catch. But in the summer, when the water level is low, it is much easier to catch them in your hands.

There are some other special places that only the boys know about. In a grove of willow trees not far from the farmhouse, the Talking Tree grows. The branches of this willow tree rub together like the strings of a violin, and Ben and Mark love to listen to the sounds they make — sometimes it sounds like music, at other times it sounds as though the tree is talking to them.

The Magic Creek is a truck ride away from the house.

Above: Ben and Mark kick puffballs and mushrooms, which grow in the paddocks in autumn. Right: Mark watches Ben and their friend Mackenzie Tapp trying to ride sheep in the shearing shed. ⬛

It became known as the Magic Creek when Ben and Mark went with their father up the creek valley to look for some missing sheep. When they came back there were Easter eggs all along the track. Ben and Mark hope to find Easter eggs at the Magic Creek every year.

Another place Ben and Mark like to go is the Secret Valley. They always find something interesting whenever they go exploring there. Their friends Fergus and Jack are the only other people who know it exists. Last time they visited the valley the boys saw a chamois, which is a type of wild goat.

On rainy days, Ben and Mark stay inside and play cards — games like poker or twenty-one — or they watch TV. In the winter it starts to get dark at four o'clock, but in the summer the evenings are long and it is still light until ten o'clock. Then they can stay outside and play soccer on the lawn. Ben and Mark say their mother is really good but she can never beat them. In the winter their father puts up goalposts so they can practise kicking their rugby ball.

Hunting is an important part of high-country life. Every station has a possum hunter who camps out in the huts, sets traps and then sells the skins of the possums he catches. Possums, which live in the native bush on Mount White, are a pest in the high country as they can infect cattle with the serious disease tuberculosis.

Like lots of high-country kids, Ben and Mark love to go hunting rabbits, hares and feral (wild) cats with their father. They are not old enough to shoot a gun but eventually he will teach them how to handle guns safety. They hunt hares and rabbits

at night by spotlight. The boys pile into their father's truck and shine the strong torch along the fencelines where the possums are usually seen. The hares run all over the paddocks.

There are other animal pests on Mount White, too. Wild deer come in close to the station's deer paddocks during the 'roar' or mating season. They will try to get through the fences to mate with the station's hinds.

When Ben and Mark go deer hunting with their father further back in the hills they have to get up very early in the morning. When they find a wild deer, their father creeps up behind it, being careful to be downwind of it so the deer cannot smell them as they get closer.

Wild pigs are also a problem in the high country, as they dig

Mark and Ben read books by the fire at the end of the day. Tui the sheep dog puppy has curled up to sleep in Mark's lap. ⊠

up the pasture with their tusks, which is known as pig rooting. Sometimes they will even attack young lambs and sheep if they find them tangled in a thorny matagouri bush.

Ben and Mark have learned to look for the telltale signs of fresh pig rooting when they go hunting with their father. Sometimes they all go out to the paddock where there is a pig trap to see if anything has been caught in it. Their father leaves a dead sheep's carcass in there to attract the big wild pigs.

Ben and Mark are always really excited when their father says it looks like a good day to go up in the plane. They can't wait to help

Above: Ben and Mark always love seeing Mount White from the air. Right: They help their father take the plane back to the hangar. 🖼

him get it out of the hangar. The plane belongs to a friend of the family and is a really handy way for their father to check the deer, cattle and sheep when he doesn't have time to ride his horse or take his truck way out into the remote areas of the station. Sometimes on Friday afternoons, if the weather is good, he flies to Springfield to pick up Ben and Mark and their mother after school.

Having a plane was also really useful the day Mark drove the little motorbike into a big patch of matagouri and couldn't get it out again. When the boys and their father all went back in the truck to get the bike out he couldn't remember where it was, and hard as they tried they couldn't see it anywhere. The next day they took the plane up and straightaway they spotted the motorbike from the air.

The plane is a very special type. It's an Auster J1Y, which was used by the Royal Air Force in the Second World War as a spotter plane.

Ben leaps off the little jetty into Lake Letitia.

FRIENDS

You might think that Mount White Station would be a lonely place because it is so far away from any other houses or towns, but in fact there are always lots of visitors.

Ben and Mark like spending time with Sonny Hodgson, who works on the station and at mustering and shearing time there are lots of other people around. Hunters and fishermen call in to the farmhouse on their way into the back country to stay at the huts. Truck drivers call in to pick up stock. Old Rusty the grader driver has spent years making the station roads safe. Ben and Mark always get a fright when their father's truck turns the corner and nearly runs into Rusty's large yellow grader.

It is true that Ben and Mark don't have other children around to play with all the time on the weekends and holidays, as children who live in towns and cities do. They have to be their own best friends and play together a lot more than many other brothers would.

However, they have good friends who live on stations nearby, and they see them whenever there is a local event or a party when they have a sleepover. Sometimes there are weddings, which are always an exciting time. In the high country, people always come

to each other's parties and because it is so far to drive back home, visitors often end up staying the night, so you get lots of time to spend together. That makes families and friends very close.

Ben and Mark's closest family friends are the Hills, the Gunns and the Tapps. The big girls of those families, Lucy Gunn and Georgie, Sarah and Charlotte Hill, love to put on plays and concerts. They all dress up and practise, then they perform for all the grown-ups, who clap and cheer.

Ben and Mark have lots of grown-up friends, too, who have known them since they were babies and have enjoyed watching them grow up. Their friend Paddy Freaney, who lives at a little village called The Bealey, on the way to Arthur's Pass, has climbed

Ben and Mark have lunch with the shearing gang in the shearing shed kitchen. ▣

FRIENDS 140

Mark drives up on his motorbike to meet his father, who
is climbing down from Ernie the big tractor. ⬈

Mount Everest. He sometimes says to the boys, 'If you think the mountains on Mount White are big, wait until you see Everest!'

Sometimes their grown-up friends take them on special trips. Murray Harford worked at Mount White for four years, as a cook, a fencer, a butcher and a musterer. He once took them to Christchurch to see a movie and they went to McDonald's twice!

Springfield School has thirty pupils and two full-time teachers. Ben and Mark really like going to school and having friends over to play after school. They also like the other things you can do in town, like going to the dairy to get an ice cream and sometimes going to the Springfield pub with their parents and having a raspberry and Coke to drink.

Although they really miss their father during the week, another thing that Ben and Mark really like about living in Springfield during the week is that they can play in a rugby team. They wouldn't be able to play any team sport if they always lived at Mount White.

Above: Mark has a raspberry and Coke at the Springfield hotel. Right: Ben and Mark with some of their friends at Springfield school. Mark's painting is of Mount White Station.

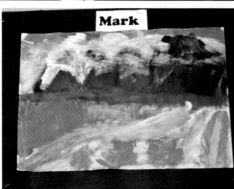

Mark

Their team practises at the next town, Sheffield, between Darfield and Springfield, and is called the Sheffield Sharks. Last year Ben and Mark both played in the same team — under eights — but next season Ben will move up a grade.

They both love rugby and support the All Blacks and the Crusaders. Mark likes Dan Carter and Ben likes Richie McCaw.

Last season Ben played at halfback, first five and number eight, and he was the top try-scorer for the team. Mark plays on the wing. There was one girl on the team, their friend Charlotte Hill, who is a really fast runner. She now goes to boarding school in Christchurch so they can't have her on the team anymore.

Ben and Mark's under-eight team the Sheffield Sharks plays Prebbleton, then the teams tuck into chips, sausage rolls and cheerios after the game.

Above and right: Ben and Mark with some of their valley friends, Fergus Gunn, Bailey Campbell and Mackenzie Tapp. Another friend, Jack Hill, is given a rough but friendly welcome on a visit to Castle Hill Station. Facing page: At the end of the Castle Hill dog trials, Ben and Mark and their friends line up for the Young Musterers' Race up to the rocks and back. Some of the girls run in fancy dress. Afterwards there's a lolly scramble.

FRIENDS 146

The bunkhouse and cookhouse photographed from the air. Ben and Mark's house is behind the pine trees to the left.

EVENTS

There's always lots going on in country districts, and in the Upper Waimakariri Valley there are some exciting events that Ben and Mark look forward to each year.

Every November in the little settlement of Cass, beside the railway line that connects the West Coast of the South Island to Christchurch, the 'Mayor of Cass', Barry Drummond, puts on an annual event on the local domain called the Cass Bash. It began thirteen years ago as a cricket game between the railway workers and 'The Valley' — the farmers, farm workers and anyone else living in the area who wanted to join in. It was six-all in the cricket series until this year, when the railway workers won. It is now seven–six. Ben and Mark's father says The Valley is going to have some serious practices before next year's match.

Ben and Mark really love the Cass Bash. Most of the grown-ups are pretty hopeless cricketers but some of them are very good and the teams are very competitive. Ben and Mark sit on the fence railings with their friends to watch. There's always a lolly scramble, too, and Ben and Mark stuff their pockets with sweets.

After the game is finished, around five o'clock, the hangi is lifted and everyone tucks in to the delicious food. The best part

of the meal is the Christmas pudding that's steamed in the hangi and then served with custard.

That night there's always a band and dancing. It's exciting running around in the dark with all your friends and getting up on the dance floor with the grown-ups.

Cass is just a tiny town but its name is well known because of a famous painting by artist Rita Angus of the railway shed that still stands there. The tourists on the TranzAlpine train across the Southern Alps love to photograph the station when the train stops at Cass.

Another big event Ben and Mark look forward to is the Malvern Agricultural and Pastoral (A&P) Show, which has been held on the Sheffield Domain for the past hundred and ten years. The show is a really special day in the district. Farmers exhibit their prize sheep, cattle and horses. There are dog trials and showjumping, merry-go-rounds and smart new tractors and harvesters on display. Ben and Mark love the hot dogs and candy floss. The children from the local schools enter the healthy lunch-box competition and the contest to make an animal out of fruit or vegetables. Last year Ben and Mark had some still-life drawings exhibited at the show.

Ben and his friend Jack Hill cheer on the cricketers and Mark grabs sweets from the lolly scramble at the Cass Bash. ◪

Cyclists and runners jostle for space when the Coast to Coast race crosses the Mount White Bridge over the Waimakariri River near Mount White Station. ⊠

Each February the famous Coast to Coast endurance race comes close to Mount White Station. The runners come out of the hills after crossing the Southern Alps from the West Coast, then jump into the kayaks waiting for them on the banks of the Waimakariri River near the Mount White Bridge. It's incredibly exciting to watch.

The first runners appear just before dawn, wearing headlamps to light their way. Ben and Mark watch as they leap into the kayaks, which have been positioned by their support crew. Some of the kayaks have bananas strapped to the sides so the competitors can eat as they paddle.

Ben and Mark go every year to watch. Their mother and father help out at the Springfield School tent, selling cooked breakfasts

to the supporters and spectators milling about. A caravan is taken down to the bridge the night before and at about four in the morning Ben and Mark's mother starts buttering loaves of bread and preparing the food. This year Ben walked around selling trays of filled rolls, raising lots of money for the school.

Ben and Mark get breakfast from their mother at the Springfield School tent and Ben sells filled rolls to a spectator. ▨

In the autumn Ben decided to enter the junior division of the Castle Hill Station dog trials with Zac. Dog trials are very tricky. The dog's owner has to use whistles to get it to round up three sheep and move them up a steep hill.

Zac and Ben did very well for their first time competing. Zac took a while to work out that Ben needed him to go after the sheep. Huntaways are meant to bark behind the sheep and send them up the hill in as straight a line as possible but Zac didn't realise he had to keep on barking. He barked a bit and then sat and looked at Ben, and the sheep moved ever so slowly up the hill. When the sheep got to the first marker posts Zac decided to lie down and have a look around.

But soon he got the idea, and Ben won the Junior Shepherd's Cup. Afterwards the judge, Jerry Roborgh, gave him some handy advice on how to make Zac follow his instructions.

Last year Mark won the Young Musterers' Race at Castle Hill. He was presented with a cup and he was so proud of it that he fell asleep in his bed with it tucked under his arm.

Last year, at the Sheffield dog trials, Mark also decided to give the musterers' race a go. He was the youngest entrant and he didn't have proper shoes on. His parents didn't know he had entered and Mark's father nearly fainted when he saw him running past. Then he started to cheer. Mark didn't win but his father was very proud of him for trying.

Above: Ben and Zac compete in Castle Hill Station's dog trials. Zac still has a lot to learn but even so Ben won the Junior Cup. Right: Afterwards, judge Jerry Roborgh (centre) and the Hills' grandfather Geoff give him some tips and then Ben sits with Jerry as he judges other entrants.

THE FUTURE

Sometimes Ben and Mark's parents wonder whether their boys will also become high-country farmers. Richard and Sheri love the farming life, but it is a very hard one. You can have a winter of kind weather and a good spring, with lots of healthy young animals and plenty of grass, but that can be followed by a dry summer. The animals will not grow as well as you had hoped and the grass will die off so there's not enough for them to eat.

You can have snow on the ground for months, or you may not get the sweet spring rains. You can enjoy years of being paid good prices for meat and wool and then there are years where the prices are low and money is tight. Animals can die, rivers may flood.

But for all those hard times, Richard and Sheri would still love their boys to go farming — to experience the wonderful freedom, to be able to walk through the tussocks and climb the high, high mountains where you feel as though you could touch the vast and wondrous sky. They would love their boys to learn how to break in a horse, to train a working dog so well that it wins its section at the local dog trials. They would love them to grow up into adulthood valuing the true friends who live in the valley, to continue to be a part of that special community. But they say that it is up to the boys to decide. They would never force them to become farmers.

To be a good farmer you have to love your stock, whether they be sheep or cows or deer. You need to have a sixth sense about the way they behave, to be always watching them and the pasture that feeds them. You need to know how to read the weather, to understand what the clouds or winds or temperature changes are telling you. You must read the markets for meat and wool and know when is the best time to sell. Sometimes even the most carefully thought-out decisions do not work out for the best and the farm doesn't produce a profit. Everyone has to hunker down and save money.

Mark is sure he wants to follow in his father's footsteps and farm in the high country. Ben is not so sure. It's a big choice for anyone to make. But Ben and Mark won't have to worry about the things their parents think about for a very long time. For now, they are two very lucky and very happy young boys of the high country.

THE END

Mark watches his father drenching the sheep. He teases Mark by pretending to give him a dose too.

THE FUTURE 166

MYSTERIOUS MOUNTAIN CREATURES

Two special kinds of sheep live in the high country, along with the more usual merinos. They are called Sidelpurgas and Hogrossnorts, and have two short legs on one side and two long legs on the other. They can only go around the hills one way, so if they miss a tasty clump of grass they have to walk all the way around again before they can stop to eat — or so Ben and Mark's father tells them!

SOME HIGH-COUNTRY TERMS

antlers — the horns of *stags*, which grow each year from the front of the deer's skull. They start as a soft growth called velvet then turn into hard bone. The deer sheds its antlers each year in the early spring, then grows a new set.

billy — a metal pot hung over an open fire to boil water for tea.

break in — to train a wild young horse to have a rider on its back.

breed — to have a baby cow, sheep or deer.

castrate — to remove a male animal's testicles so it can't breed, normally done when the animal is young.

Clydesdale — a breed of large, powerful horse bred for farm work and pulling loads.

crutching — the removal of wool from the bottom of a sheep, so it stays clean.

dags — lumps of matted and soiled wool around a sheep's bottom.

dipping — spraying animals with a medicine to prevent problems such as fly strike.

drenching — putting medicine down the throat of an animal to kill parasites such as worms.

ear-tagging — attaching a plastic tag to an animal's ear so it can be identified. Sometimes notches are cut into the ear instead. This is called ear-marking.

ewe — a mature female sheep, usually after two years of age.

eye dog — see *heading dog*.

fawn — a baby deer.

feeding out — giving animals *hay* or silage in winter and in dry weather when there isn't enough fresh grass for them to eat.

fly strike — when flies lay their eggs on the skin and wool of a sheep and the eggs hatch into maggots, causing the sheep pain and distress.

foot rot — a disease in the feet of sheep and other hoofed animals, caused by bacteria. It is particularly common with merino sheep and causes pain and lameness.

gang — a group of musterers, shearers or workers on a farm.

hack — a big, strong, reliable horse bred especially for riding in the rough high country.

hands — a unit of measurement of the height of a horse, measured from the ground to the top of its shoulders.

handy dog — a general-purpose dog that can do all the duties required of dogs in sheep yards and woolsheds. More specialised dogs are called heading dogs and huntaways.

hay — grass or other crops such as lucerne or oats that have been mown, dried and baled to be used for feeding out.

heading dog — a dog that herds sheep by staring at them rather than barking at them. Also called an *eye dog*.

Hereford — a type of cattle bred for its meat, originally from Hereford in England.

high-country station — a very large farm, at an altitude of above 1000 metres above sea level, usually carrying fine-wool sheep such as merinos, along with cattle and deer.

hind — a female deer.

home paddocks — the flat land around the farmhouse where many animals are kept during winter.

huntaway — a special type of sheep dog used for mustering. These dogs make the sheep move by barking on command.

imprinting — handling an animal when it is very young so it gets used to being touched by people.

mare — an adult female horse or pony.

matagouri — a thorny native shrub that grows in the high country.

merino — a special type of hardy sheep with beautiful soft wool. It prefers to live in the dry mountains and hills of the South Island high country.

mustering — gathering or collecting animals together. The men and women who do this job are called musterers.

packie — the member of the mustering gang who does all the cooking and moves the team's food and sleeping gear from hut to hut during the muster.

ram – an adult male sheep that has not been castrated, so is able to breed.

rouseabout — a worker helping out in a shearing shed.

scree — the loose shingle that streams down the slopes of the South Island mountains.

silage — grass or other crops such as lucerne or oats that have been mown and compacted with heavy machinery into a stack or pit and covered with plastic, to be used for feeding out.

smoko — a morning or afternoon tea break.

stag — adult male deer.

steer — a male cow that has been castrated, so it can't breed.

tailing — removing a large part of a young animal's tail to stop droppings sticking to it. Also called docking.

tuberculosis — a serious disease in cattle that is spread in New Zealand mostly by possums.

tussock — a native grass that grows throughout the high country.

weaner — a young animal that has been separated from its mother and no longer drinks milk.

wether — a male sheep that has been castrated so it can't *breed*.

ACKNOWLEDGEMENTS

They say you can take a person from the high country but you can't take the high country out of the person. John and I believe this saying; the high country is certainly under our skins, so pervasive and glorious are the land and the sky and the high-country people.

Richard and Sheri are the essence of the high-country spirit. They are a remarkable couple, grand custodians of the majesty that is Mount White Station. Thank you Richard and Sheri for allowing John to range all over the station, in and out of your home and buildings, dragging the boys this way and that. Thank you, too, for answering a million questions and trusting me to write a story that is both personal and forever.

To the Turnbull family, the owners of Mount White: thank you for sharing your paradise with us. How fortunate that Mount White has been owned for eighty years by a family prepared to take the good years with the bad and who love this part of New Zealand's high country.

To Imogen Tunnicliffe, thank you for the lovely maps of the station and the illustrations of the Sidelpurgas and Hogrossnorts.

At Random House, thanks to Nicola Legat, who in the most subtle and persuasive way gets the best out of writers, photographers and illustrators, and to Anna Seabrook for the charming book design.